For all the four-footed creatures we love
—E.L.

To Jeni. Thank you for teaching me about horses.
—K.H.

Text copyright © 2022 by Elizabeth Letts
Jacket art and interior illustrations copyright © 2022 by Kayla Harren

This work is based on *The Eighty-Dollar Champion: Snowman, the Horse That Inspired a Nation,* copyright © 2011 by Elizabeth Letts. Published in hardcover in the United States by Ballantine, an imprint of Random House, a division of Penguin Random House LLC, New York, in 2011.

Visit us on the Web! rhcbooks.com

Educators and librarians, for a variety of teaching tools, visit us at RHTeachersLibrarians.com

Library of Congress Cataloging-in-Publication Data is available upon request.
ISBN 978-0-593-17385-5 (trade) — ISBN 978-0-593-17386-2 (lib. bdg.) —
ISBN 978-0-593-17387-9 (ebook)

MANUFACTURED IN CHINA
10 9 8 7 6 5 4 3 2 1
First Edition

My Blue-Ribbon Horse

The True Story of The Eighty-Dollar Champion

by Elizabeth Letts

illustrated by Kayla Harren

Random House ⌂ New York

Harry de Leyer was a horseback-riding teacher at a school for girls. He was on his way to a horse sale, hoping to find a well-behaved animal to buy. But he was running late. Would all the horses be sold?

When Harry arrived, the sale was already over. One truck remained, but the driver was ready to leave.

Harry peered through the truck's sides. A big white horse huddled up against the boards. The poor creature was dirty and run-down, yet had a gentle look in his eye.

"What are you going to do with him?" Harry asked.

He already knew the answer. Harry's stomach knotted in frustration. He thought horses who were past their prime should be allowed to retire to green pastures with tender grass.

Harry's fingers clutched the money he'd brought to the sale. Harry knew he shouldn't spend it on a neglected animal. The riding students at his school liked fancy horses who could jump high. Surely this old horse would never be able to jump.

The horse pointed his ears forward and stretched out his thin neck.

"How much do you want for him?" Harry asked.

"Oh, you don't need this one," the man replied gruffly.

"I can pay eighty dollars," Harry said.

The man grinned and accepted. He promised to drop off the horse at Harry's barn later that day.

Back home, Harry told his wife, Johanna, and their children about the new member of the family. Their daughter, Harriet, was excited. "He's a bit skinny and worn out," her father warned, "but he's a good horse."

The family worked together to get a home ready for him. They poured fresh oats and filled a stall with straw to make a soft bed.

It was past dark when the truck rattled into the driveway. When the horse
saw Harry, he whinnied. Harriet hoped he would notice her.

She didn't need to worry. As soon as he got out of
the truck, the gentle giant peered at her. Fat snowflakes
fell from the sky, covering the mud stains on his back.
"Why don't we call him Snowman?" Harriet said.

Every day, Harriet went to visit Snowman in the family's barn. When her father wasn't busy, he let Harriet sit on Snowman's back.

But the girls at the school liked other horses better. They wanted to ride horses who could jump.

Even though the family loved Snowman, Harry would have to find him a new home. He wouldn't be able to jump in competitions, and it was too expensive to keep him as a pet.

One day when Harriet visited the stable, a boy was riding Snowman.

His father gave Harry some crisp bills, and the boy took Snowman away. Harriet missed his warm brown eyes, his gentle whinnies, and the soft whiskers on his nose.

"Don't be sad," Harry said to Harriet. "We found a good home for him." Harriet knew her father was right, but she still missed the big white horse.

A few days later, what a surprise! Snowman was back, standing next to his stall with a twinkle in his eye. *Where had he come from?*

Snowman had jumped a pasture fence and galloped all the way home. "This won't do," Harry said. "He needs to go back to the boy who bought him."

But Snowman came back again the next day, and again and again.

He couldn't bear to stay away from the family who had saved him.

Now Harry had a new idea.... If Snowman could jump high fences, maybe Harry could train him to jump competitively. He could enter Snowman in a show and maybe even win a prize.

Every day, Harry trained Snowman. But with these lower fences,
Snowman almost didn't bother to pick up his feet. He stumbled
and knocked down the poles every time.

Harry was puzzled. Why was Snowman so clumsy over these small jumps? The pasture fence was almost as high as Harry's shoulders. Maybe Snowman liked to jump higher. Harry would give it a try.

Harry crouched forward and galloped the horse toward a high hurdle. Harry whispered a word of encouragement and held the reins steady.

One, two, three strides, up, up, up, he soared. Harry felt as if they were floating on air. Now Harry understood the puzzle.

Every day, they practiced in the school's riding arena. Every day, Harry added another bar to the fence. Every day, Snowman soared over the fence with ease.

After a few months, Harry believed Snowman was ready. He wanted to enter him in a show.

The whole family worked to prepare the horse. Snowman had never looked better.

But what would people think? Snowman would be competing against fancy Thoroughbreds who cost thousands of dollars. And to win the blue ribbon, the horse had to clear every fence without knocking down a single pole.

Harry and Snowman entered the arena. Snowman's coat glowed. His tail was shiny and silver. But some people laughed. They thought he didn't belong.

"Come on, Snowy!" Harry whispered.

Harry and Snowman circled the arena at a gallop. As they got close to each fence, Snowman gathered his legs underneath him and leapt high into the air, snapping up his knees to clear the obstacle with room to spare.

The people who had laughed at Snowman were quiet now, watching the big horse's performance with surprise.

Snowman and Harry cleared the last fence without knocking down a single pole. They had done it! They had captured the silver trophy and the blue ribbon!

After that, Harry and Snowman were unstoppable. The de Leyer family took Snowman to all the biggest horse shows. Newspapers loved to write about the eighty-dollar horse beating the expensive Thoroughbreds. And at each show, Snowman won more and more fans. He continued to compete for several years, winning trophies, ribbons, accolades, and love from the entire world. Snowman wasn't a failure anymore. He was a champion.

AUTHOR'S NOTE

Harry de Leyer was born in St. Oedenrode, the Netherlands, in 1928. After World War II, he and his wife, Johanna, immigrated to the United States. Harry and Johanna worked hard and built a good life for themselves and their eight children. In 1956, Harry went to the New Holland horse auction in the Amish Country of Pennsylvania, intending to buy a horse for his pupils to learn to jump. Harry arrived so late that all the horses had been sold except the ones on their way to a slaughterhouse. He took pity on a weathered white horse and decided to purchase him for eighty dollars.

Harry and his family cared for the horse, but his pupils didn't want to ride Snowman, and he was expensive to maintain as a pet. Harry sold him to a neighbor—and the horse kept jumping pasture fences to gallop the three miles back to Harry's barn. Realizing that Snowman might have potential as a jumper, after all, Harry decided to train him.

Within two years, he was unstoppable—he was the national show jumping champion in 1958 and 1959. Nicknamed the Cinderella Horse, Snowman became the most celebrated horse of his time.

Even though Snowman was financially valuable because of his competition wins, Harry turned down multiple offers to buy the horse. He retired Snowman in 1962 to live out his days in peace at Harry's Hollandia Farms. In years to come, their many fans called Harry the Galloping Grandfather. He spent his later years watching horses out his windows. Harry passed away peacefully at the age of 93 in 2021.